ISBN 978-1-332-11431-3
PIBN 10286552

English
Français
Deutsche
Italiano
Español
Português

www.forgottenbooks.com

Mythology Photography **Fiction**
Fishing Christianity **Art** Cooking
Essays Buddhism Freemasonry
Medicine **Biology** Music **Ancient
Egypt** Evolution Carpentry Physics
Dance Geology **Mathematics** Fitness
Shakespeare **Folklore** Yoga Marketing
Confidence Immortality Biographies
Poetry **Psychology** Witchcraft
Electronics Chemistry History **Law**
Accounting **Philosophy** Anthropology
Alchemy Drama Quantum Mechanics
Atheism Sexual Health **Ancient History**
Entrepreneurship Languages Sport
Paleontology Needlework Islam
Metaphysics Investment Archaeology
Parenting Statistics Criminology
Motivational

COLONEL NINIAN BEALL

Born in Largo, Fifeshire, Scotland, 1625,
Died in Prince George's County, Maryland, 1717.

Historical Address on the
Occasion of the Dedication
of a Memorial Boulder to
Colonel Ninian Beall
Delivered by
Caleb Clarke Magruder, Jr.
in St. John's Church,
Georgetown, D. C.,
Sunday, October 30, 1910.

Printed under the auspices of
The Society of Colonial Wars in the District of Columbia
January 27, 1911

INTRODUCTION.

IN the summer of 1909 the finding of a large boulder in a cut on the line of the Metropolitan Southern railway near the junction of the right of way with the Glen Echo railway was communicated to Dr. Marcus Benjamin and by him promptly referred to Mr. William Van Zandt Cox, then Governor of the Society of Colonial Wars in the District of Columbia.

Appreciating the fact that this boulder might be used to preserve the memory of Colonel Joseph Belt whose career had been so fully presented to the Society in a valuable paper* by our Historian, Mr. Cox at once appointed a Committee on Memorials, as follows: Mr. Thomas Hyde, chairman, Mr. Caleb C. Magruder, Jr., Judge Job Barnard, Dr. Marcus Benjamin, and Mr. William S. Knox. The Committee was quickly convened by its chairman and their first efforts were directed toward securing formal possession of this valuable find. The rock was inspected by members of the Committee who found to their great satisfaction that since it had blocked the progress of the contractor he had so blasted it as to make two boulders of nearly equal size. Through the courtesy of Mr. George E. Hamilton, local attorney for the Metropolitan Southern railway, permission was given to the Committee to remove the boulders. They were accordingly placed in the vicinity of Chevy Chase Circle where they remained until authority was given to the Committee for final action.

In the autumn the Chairman of the Committee made

---

*Historical Paper, No. 5, Colonel Joseph Belt. By Caleb Clarke Magruder, Jr., with Patent and illustration of Chevy Chase manor-house, pp. 36. 1909.

a verbal report to the Society recommending that one boulder be placed near Chevy Chase Circle to commemorate the services of Colonel Joseph Belt, and that the other be erected in Georgetown as a memorial to Colonel Ninian Beall, whose association during the Colonial period with the province of Maryland now included in the District of Columbia, had previously been interestingly described in a paper read before the Society by Mr. Zebina Moses and later privately published by him.

This report was approved by the Society and the Committee was authorized to have the boulders placed in suitable localities. The Committee visited various eligible sites, and finally decided to place one boulder at the northwest corner of the parking facing All Saints' Church, at the junction of the Belt Road and Connecticut Avenue, Chevy Chase, south of Grafton street and just within the District line.

The other boulder was erected at the southeast corner of O and Potomac streets on the grounds of St. John's Church, Georgetown, D. C. It was also recommended that the boulder in memory of Colonel Beall be dedicated in the autumn of 1910, and that to Colonel Joseph Belt at a date to be decided upon later. It is hoped that these granite boulders commemorating the life and works of worthy colonial heroes may serve to testify to the high respect and esteem with which their memory is preserved by loyal descendants in the Society of Colonial Wars.

There remains only to add that because of the interest of a descendant of Colonel Ninian Beall, a member of the local Society, an appropriate bronze tablet was obtained and placed on the boulder in Georgetown. An account of the exercises that formed a part of the dedication ceremony is also included in this pamphlet.

THE CEREMONIES.

WHEN information came to the Committee that the bronze tablet for the Ninian Beall memorial bearing an inscription prepared by the Historian, was approaching completion Justice Barnard, Governor of the District Society, appointed a committee consisting of Dr. Marcus Benjamin, Mr. Zebina Moses, and Mr. Frederick D. Owen to arrange for the dedicatory ceremonies. The general preparation of the program was undertaken by the Chairman, while to Mr. Moses was assigned the care of the church, and to Mr. Owen, whose skill in similar functions is so favorably known, was given the charge of the outdoor exercises of the unveiling.

The day selected was the last Sunday in October, and shortly before four o'clock in the afternoon the members, wearing the insignia of the Society, gathered in the rooms of the Parish House and then at the appointed time, preceded by the standard bearers carrying the flag of the Society and the Nation's colors, and led by Governor Barnard, followed by former governors, and officers, and then the members, marched into the church.

Scarcely had they taken the places assigned to them when the organ broke forth with the music of the processioual hymn:

"Ancient of days, who sittest throned in glory;
To Thee all knees are bent, all voices pray."

Following the choristers, chanting the sacred words, came the clergy, including the Reverend Doctor Roland Cotton Smith, Chaplain of the Society; the Reverend Frederick B. Howden, rector of St. John's; Archdeacon

(5)

Richard P. Williams; and the Right Reverend Alfred Harding, Bishop of Washington.

Then came the Choral Even Song, the Rector officiating, and the lesson from the Epistle to the Hebrews being read by Archdeacon Williams. The Prayers included the following one specially prepared for the Society of Colonial Wars:

O God, who hast promised in Thy Holy Word to show mercy unto generation after generation of those who love Thee, and keep Thy commandments. We give Thee hearty thanks for the good examples of all those Thy servants who bore faithful witness for true religion and Christian freedom in the days of our forefathers. And we humbly beseech Thee to continue Thy protection to their children, and especially to the members of the Society of Colonial Wars. Strengthen them to be defenders of their country's Godly heritage, and mercifully grant that all things in this, our Fatherland, may be so ordered and settled upon the best and surest foundations, that peace and happiness, truth and justice, religion and piety, may be established among us for all generations. All of which we ask through Jesus Christ our Lord.

At the close of the Service the choristers sang the martial hymn:

"The Son of God goes forth to war,
A kingly crown to gain."

Then came the address of Mr. Caleb C. Magruder, Jr., the Historian of the Society, which appears elsewhere in this pamphlet.

The anthem by Naylor followed, the opening sentence being: "Behold, God is great, and we know Him not, the number of His years is unsearchable."

The Society, with its flags, then passed from the church, and, with the clergy, assembled about the memorial boulder. The Chaplain of the Society conducted the outdoor service, which began with the following exhortation:

Good People, We are gathered together in the Name and Presence of Almighty God, to dedicate a memorial of the noble works of which we have heard with our ears, and our fathers have declared unto us that God did then in their days and in the old time before them. For they got not the land in possession through their own sword, neither was it their own arm that helped them; but God's right hand, and God's arm, and the light of God's countenance, because He did a favour unto them. Wherefore I beseech you to call upon God our Father, through our Lord Jesus Christ, that he would assist us in this our present undertaking, and in all other works undertaken for the glory of God and the good of this nation.

This was followed by proper prayers including the Collect for the Society of Colonial Wars.

The memorial was then unveiled by the following members of the Society, descendants of Colonel Ninian Beall: William M. Beall, J. Malcolm Henry, J. William Henry, Thomas Hyde, Caleb C. Magruder, Jr., Dr. Steuart B. Muncaster, Dr. Henderson Suter, and Dr. Walter A. Wells. After which the memorial was dedicated with the following words:

On behalf of the vestry of St. John's Church, Georgetown Parish, in the Diocese of Washington, I do dedicate this boulder, erected by the Society of Colonial Wars in the District of Columbia, to the memory of Ninian Beall. We yield Thee hearty thanks most merciful Father, that it hast pleased Thee to place among men Thy servant of strong arm and Christian voice whose works helped to make possible the building of our nation and the spread of Thy teachings. We thank Thee also for those of his children who have followed in his pathway of Christian religion and civic virtue. And humbly we beseech Thee to grant, that by Thy grace, all his worthy qualities may be born again in each succeeding generation to the glory of Thy Holy Name and the perpetuation of our country, through Jesus Christ our Lord.

The service concluded with a benediction by the Right Reverend Alfred Harding, Bishop of Washington. Distinct features of the occasion were the choral service under the direction of Organist and Choirmaster Williams, and the presence of numerous descendants of Colonel Beall, many of them members of American Clan Gregor, as were also members of the District of Columbia Society of Colonial Dames, and members of the Club of Colonial Dames, both of which organizations were officially invited to be present.

Colonel Ninian Beall.

By Caleb Clarke Magruder, Jr.

WHEN its travail is past and its young growth attained nations are wont to indulge in retrospection. This world-old custom gives rise to patriotism and the writing of history.

These twin subjects stimulate similar efforts, for "History is past politics," and genealogy is past personal history.

Among the resultants have been the erection of monuments, the placing of tablets, and the setting of boulders.

Such is a most wholesome custom for by them we make live again the deeds of our heroes, acknowledge the priceless heritages bequeathed us, and blazon in the paths of youth those qualities which in perpetuation shall preserve "us a nation."

And so with these three-fold desires it is a happy occasion which brings us together in the waning shadows of this holy afternoon, for we are met to record in bronze on everlasting rock the deeds of a conspicuous factor in Colonial days.

The boulder set in the Cathedral Close to mark the route of Braddock's march against Fort Duquesne stands as the first memorial of a local colonial event, and the boulder we shall soon unveil will stand as the first commemorative of a local Colonial personage.

Therefore it is with a measure of pardonable pride that the Society of Colonial Wars in the District of Columbia greets their friends in this hour of another successful endeavor in patriotic duty and personal gratification.

The inscription on yonder tablet is a concise statement of many winnowed facts. It is my pleasant task to be more diffuse, and recount services—military, civil, and secular—so that knowing them, and remembering the period of his activity, we may all the better appreciate that this memorial stands not only for the man, but for all the noble qualities which were his.

⟩ Ninian Beall was born in Largo, Fifeshire, Scotland, in 1625. He was a loyal Scot and cornet under the banner of Leslie who was routed by Cromwell and Monk at the battle of Dunbar in 1650.

Taken prisoner there he was transported to Barbadoes and thence to Maryland, where he settled in Calvert County about 1655, certainly as early as 1658.

A victim of the fortunes of war he was sentenced to five years in bondage—an honorable servitude—and that he performed its requirements honestly and faithfully is evidenced by the Provincial records of January 16, 1667, reading: "Then came Ninian Beale of Calvert County, Planter, and proved right to 50 acres of land for his time service performed with Richard Hall of same county."

Ninian Beall's earliest activity in Indian affairs is suggested in an order of May 16, 1676, emanating from the Lord-Proprietor and his Council, by whom he was summoned to appear before them to testify regarding the murder of five Susquehannocks.

The Navigation Act, passed in 1645, and many times

THE FINDING OF THE BOULDERS.

reenacted, restricted the carrying of exports and imports on English bottoms between the mother-country and the colonies, and was the cause of pronounced complaint in Maryland and Virginia.

So great became the discontent in the latter province that hostilities began under Nathaniel Bacon—the first American Rebel—in 1676, just one hundred years before the signing of an instrument whose spirit of defiance inspired a type which made revolution possible.

Fearing the revolt might assume large proportions in Maryland, where an armed force under Davis and Pate had already assembled in Calvert County, Governor Thomas Notley ordered the "Loyall Charles of Maryland," Lord Baltimore's "Yacht or vessel of warr" to cruise in the waters adjacent to Virginia under command of Captain John Coode and Ninian Beall whom he named as Lieutenant on November 8, 1676. "And I Doe hereby constitute and appoint Ninion Beal, your Lievetenant in said Yacht or Vessell, who is hereby also authorized and empowered to act doe and performe in all thinges as your Lievetenant, as amply fully and largely to all intents and purposes as if he had read a Speciall Commission drawne to that purpose."

Fortunately at least for the peace of the two colonies Bacon's meteoric career ended within a few months—some authorities say by poison—when Davis and Pate paid the penalty of insurrection with their lives.

There seems to be no record of Ninian Beall as a private soldier, but doubtless his military experiences in Scotland had prepared him for immediate martial leadership in the new world.

The policy of Maryland settlers was always one of

equity and good will toward the Indians, which bore fruit in kindly reciprocal action.

There were long the isolated murder and occasional attack expected of savage natures, some times inspired by the evil influence of rival parties, but the colony never experienced such massacres the descriptions of which form bloody pages in the history of sister colonies.

The Patuxents, the Piscataways, and the Choptanks were early friends. The Nanticokes and Susquehannocks were more ferocious, but the former were soon tamed, and the latter were forced to friendliness as a matter of self-preservation from their ancient enemies the Senecas and the Oneidas.

Notwithstanding such occasional disturbances only the possibilities of greater dangers existed. Realizing these a most thorough system of ranging throughout the borders of the province was inaugurated by Ninian Beall, and we can recall no equally preventive measure under the leadership of one so seemingly well acquainted with Indian nature.

On the 10th of August, 1678, Lieutenant Beall, now for the first time styled Captain, was ordered to range about the head of the Patuxent River to insure the safety and defense of the neighboring plantations, but to offer no violence unless provoked.

The diligence and thoroughness with which this duty was performed, and the appreciation of Lord Baltimore and his Council is indicated by a subsequent commission "by his Lordship's especiall command," carrying the exercise of broad military discretion in these words:

"You are hereby Authorized and Empowered Upon any occasion of Indians comeing into your parts, or other

emergent business, to press a mann and horse to give what speedy Intelligence thereof possible you cann to his Ldsp, for which this shall be your Sufficient Warrant. Dated at St Maries the 13th Day of January Anno Dmi 1681.
Signed p order and appointment of the Rt honble the Lord Propry
                                    p   John Llewellen
                                             cl cousil
        To Captain Ninian Beale
           These''

The exact date of his promotion to the rank of Major is not of record, but he held such rank March 24, 1689, when he was ordered by Henry Jowles, Colonel of Calvert County, to hold his command in readiness to learn the attitude of the Indians prior to the outbreak of the revolution of that year.

The basic events which led to the Revolution of 1689 were a series of unfortunate and unpreventable circumstances. Because of them the Lord-Proprietor was robbed of his inherited Charter rights, and the people deprived of that freedom of conscience through religious exercises always theirs but more specifically proclaimed in the Toleration Act of 1649. By this act Maryland became "The Land of Sanctuary," and as such stood unique and alone among the thirteen colonies.

In 1684 George Talbot, a kinsman of Lord Baltimore, boarded a ship of the King's navy used to collect custom duties. Among the crew was Christopher Rousby, a notorious character one of the King's collectors. While in a drunken condition Rousby insulted and attempted to assault Talbot, who stabbed him to death. Shortly after John Payne, another collector, was killed in a private brawl.

James II having been forced to abdicate his throne in favor of his daughter Mary in 1688, Lord Baltimore immediately dispatched a messenger to the Council with instructions to proclaim William and Mary as rightful sovereigns, but the messenger died before landing. Other colonies proclaimed the new rulers but the Council of Maryland awaited instructions.

The cry arose that the crown was being robbed of its just custom dues, that the Proprietary government was unfriendly to William and Mary, who were Protestants, and that the Catholics were bent on restoring King James to the throne. The movement was not at first popular, but owing to ignorance of affairs because of scattered habitations religious prejudices were aroused by alleged plottings and murder.

John Coode, who gained an unenviable prominence because of his connection with Fendall's rebellion in his effort to overthrow Lord Baltimore's government in 1659, raised the standard of revolt as the protector of the Protestants and the representative of King William. An association being formed with Coode as its head they marched to St. Mary's and dispersed the Council.

Lord Baltimore's adherents under Colonel Henry Darnall engarrisoned themselves at Mattapany but were shortly outnumbered and surrounded. Finding further resistance could only lead to the sacrifice of many lives they received articles of surrender signed by Coode, Ninian Beall, and others. Forced to capitulate on the offered terms all their arms and ammunition were surrendered to Colonel Henry Darnall and Major Ninian Beall.

The immediate result was the formation of a Protestant Association by which Coode was made Commander-in-

Chief of military forces and the governing head of civil affairs with Ninian Beall as a leading assistant in both branches of government. King William was petitioned to take possession of the colony, which he speedily did and sent out Sir Lionel Copley as governor in 1691. Maryland thus became a Royal Colony and so continued for twenty-five years, although Lord Baltimore's charter was permitted to remain in force.

Coode proved himself a high-handed tyrant in many ways, particularly in his restrictions toward the Catholics, and made the blackest page in Maryland history.

The Revolution of 1689 was the greatest upheaval, civilly and religiously, in Maryland from the time of the planting of the colony until the outbreak of the Revolutionary war. Apart from the circumstances before mentioned it is almost incredible that such a despicable character as Coode could involve so many substantial men in the vortex of his ambitions. That the reports concerning plots between Catholics and Indians to murder Protestants was without foundation is evidenced by a letter written March 27, 1689, and signed by many representative men of the province, among them Ninian Beall.

One of the early acts of the Council in 1692 was the establishment of the Church of England as the state church of the colony, a measure favored by Ninian Beall, although he was a Presbyterian.

The popularity and prestige of the promoters of the Revolution was short-lived, Coode in particular falling into quick disfavor. He reappeared again in 1696, when he was elected a Burgess from St. Mary's County, but Governor Nicholson, backed by his council, refused to administer the oath of office to him, asserting that as an apostate he was debarred by the laws of England from membership in a legislative body.

Coode offered to foreswear his ordination. The House of Burgesses, actuated more by a determination to maintain their prerogatives than by regard for the man, declared their right to be judges of the qualifications of their own members and insisted on his membership. Governor Nicholson was as "A Head of Iron," and when he added blasphemy to the charge of apostasy the House took counsel with itself, and endorsed his stand.

Coode immediately sought to overthow the government he had been prominent in establishing, but his character was too well known, and as a discredited alarmist, he was forced to flee the colony. He afterward returned and was pardoned, an example of maudlin magnanimity. This episode is the origin of the organic law of Maryland which prohibits any clergyman being a member of her legislature, the only one of our states with such a legal inhibition.

When Sir Francis Nicholson became Governor, he issued a proclamation over date of July 27, 1694, continning in service all military and civil officers holding commissions under his predecessor's Council by whom Major Ninian Beall had been made Colonel and Commander-in-Chief of all their Majesty's forces or militia of horse and foot in Calvert County, October 29, 1692.

On the 9th of October, 1694, the militia of the province was reorganized and special colors designated for horse, foot, and dragoon of the several counties. St. Mary's was assigned red; Anne Arundel, white; Kent, blue. This accidental distribution of colors, red, white and blue to the three oldest counties of Maryland in the order of their formation seems a most significant happening. George Washington, from whose arms our national emblem is derived, was yet unborn, and Lexington was four-score years in the womb of time.

"When I dipt into the future far as human eye could see!
Saw the vision of the world, and all the wonder that would be."

By this reorganization Henry Jowles succeeded Ninian Beall as Colonel of Calvert County. At the same time "It being Represented in Councill that Colonell Ninian Beale has allways been a person very ready & Serviceable upon comotions or insurrections made by Indians and that he is seated convenient at the head of Patuxent River to give notice and raise Men upon all such incident and Emergent occasions—And for as much as his Majties by his Royall Instruction to his Execncy has Comanded that fitting officers should be Appointed at the heads of Rivers to the Sd End & purpose Ordered thereupon that Sd Colonell Beale have a particular Comission for his Excency to raise and Comand what Men he thinkes fit in all the neighborhood in those parts upon all Occasions of such Comotion & insurrection so soone as the same shall come to his knowledge."

In accordance with the Council's recommendation the following order issued:

"I doe hereby Authorize and Empower Collonell Ninian Beale to Execute all the powers According to the above Order of myself and their Majties Honoble Councell, for wch this shall be his Comission.

Given under my hand & Seale this 18th day of Octobr Annoq Dom: 1694 in the Sixth Yeare of their Majties Reigne

ffracs Nicholson [Seal.]"

On August 17, 1695, a new county was ordered erected in the province to be known as Prince George's in honor of Prince George of Denmark, prince consort, whose colors should be the flag of St. George, our Society's flag, a red cross on a white field.

The functions of county government began on April 23d, 1696, St. George's Day, an explanation for the county sometimes being referred to in the older records as St. George's. The seat of government was located at Mount Calvert on the Patuxent River; and it was further ordered by the Council that the public building should be so constructed as to serve for the court house and church. This precedence of Mount Calvert was of short duration, the county-seat being moved to Upper Marlborough in 1706. The new county of Prince George's consisted of four hundreds—Patuxent, Collington, Mount Calvert, and Mattapany with a total of 514 taxables. William Hatton was named as Chief-Justice with directions to use his private seal for that of the court until one was adopted. William Cooper was clerk of the court, and John Addison, great-great-grandfather of the founder of this church, Reverend Walter Dulany Addison, colonel of militia.

Colonel Ninian Beall and Major William Barton having been elected the first Burgesses they were inducted into office on May 11, 1696, the service of the former extending through five years. Hardly had he entered upon his duties before he was excused by the Assembly to inquire into the causes of some Indian alarms.

In 1697 he was one of a committee to secure peaceful assurances from the Nanticokes and Piscataways. In view of their unrest it was thought wise to ask the cooperation of Colonel Beall notwithstanding he was no longer Colonel of the county, so that Colonel Addison was ordered to "discourse" Colonel Beall to ascertain

if he was still willing to continue in the commission he held for raising men upon any Indian disturbances.

Learning the desire of the Council Colonel Beall promptly offered his services to command one party of the new Rangers to be raised along the "Potomak;" whereupon that body replied Colonel Beale "is well accepted of by this board."

During the sessions of 1698 he was a member of the committee on Laws and the committee to examine the accounts of Robert Mason, Treasurer of the Western Shore. In the mid-fall of the same year he signed a testimonial of personal regard and acknowledgment of a beneficial administration to Sir Francis Nicholson, who was leaving Maryland to become for the second time Governor of Virginia.

Sir Francis was the founder of William and Mary College, Williamsburg, Va., in 1693, after Harvard the oldest college in the United States, and of King William's School, now St. John's College, Annapolis, Maryland, the first free school in Maryland, and the third oldest college in the United States. This zealous worker in the cause of education in two provinces deserves a memorial in their halls of fame. Appreciating his efforts Maryland has placed a tablet to his memory in Baltimore.

In 1699 Colonel Beall represented the House of Burgesses on a committee appointed by the Assembly to investigate Indian affairs with such a marked degree of satisfaction that he was, on July 14, 1699, made Commander-in-Chief of Rangers or Provincial forces, the supreme military command in the province.

Seemingly not content with conferring this distinguished honor the Council, with the concurrence of

Governor Nathaniel Blackiston, directed this memorial to the House of Burgesses: "The consideration of this subject [Indian affairs] brings into remembrance the many Signall Services and Laborious Endeavours of Col Ninian Beal one of your Members which he still Continues Willingly Even beyond what his age seems capable of; And that good Services may not go unrewarded and others in time to Come Encouraged thereby to Exert their Abilitys in the Country Service It is recommended to your Consideration to make him some Allowance out of the public Stock to the Value of a hundred pounds or so much money as will buy him four Negros and that Some person may be Appointed to buy and deliver them to him and that they may be Settled in Some person for his use and Supporte during his life and after during his Wife's and after to such Child or Children as he shall depose by his last will and testamt. and not Subject to payment of any the said Beal's Debts."

This recommendation echoed a most pronounced sentiment of regard for Colonel Beall entertained by his fellow-members of the House of Burgesses.

A bill was immediately drafted and after the required readings the Assembly passed "An Act of Gratuity:"

"Whereas Colonell Ninian Beal has been found very Serviceable to this Province upon all Incursions and Disturbances of Neighbouring Indians and though now grown very Aged and less able to performe, Yet Continnes his Resolution even beyond his Ability to do the line Service att this Juncture of Affaires it is therefore thought fitt in Point of Gratitude, for Such his good service done and towards his Supporte & Reliefe now in his old age to make him an Allowance out of the Publick Revenue of this Province Be it therefore Enacted by the Kings most Excellent Maty by and with the Advice and Consent of this present General Assembly and the Authority of the Same, That Mr William Hutchison a Member of this house as a Trustee for and on the behalfe of the said Col Ninian Beal hath hereby Given to him full power and Authority to Procure and Purchase three good Serviceable Negro Slaves for the Proper use and benefitt of him the said Colo Ninian Beal for and during his Naturall life and after his decease to the use of his wife during her Naturall life and after her decease then the said Negros & Slaves and their Encrease to the Sole use and Benefitt of their Child or Children according to the request or Devise of him the said Ninion Beal by will or otherwise and for that end and purpose the said William Hutchison hath hereby full power and Authority to draw a Bill or Bills for the Sume of Seventy five pound Sterling upon the Treasurer of the Western Shoar Who is likewise hereby required to Yield and Pay the Same out of the Public Stock of this Province for which he shall be Allowed and have Creditt in his Acct currant att the Rendring thereof as p Act of Assembly he is obliged And be it further Enacted by the Authority aforesaid by and with the Advice and Concent aforesaid That the said Negroes and their Increase Shall not dureing the life of the said Ninian Beal or his wife be taken in Execution for any Judgement or Attachment Whatsoever Obtained or hereafter to be obtained any Law Statute or usage to the Contrary in any wise Notwithstanding.''

The exact date of its final passage is unknown but Colonel Beall acknowledged receipt of the three slaves— John, Sarah, and Elizabeth—May 28, 1699.

This act is the superlative formal expression of appreciation and reward passed in favor of an individual during Colonial times—a period of one hundred and forty-two years.

There is an apparent discourtesy to one of their members by the House of Burgesses in reducing the amount of the gratuity from one hundred pounds sterling to seventy-five pounds sterling as proposed by the Council. It is more apparent than real however when we recall that the House of Burgesses represented the people and were the guardians of the purse-strings of the province. Moreover they purposed by such action to impress upon the Council their absolute freedom and liberty of action for which they were accountable to the people only and by which they sowed the seed of future independence.

An old settlement account dated February 6, 1700, shows Colonel Beall had ranged 241 days for which his allowance was forty pounds three shillings four pence, a daily rate of less than three hundred dollars a year.

The year 1700 saw his last service in the House of Burgesses, and one might naturally think that with the weight of seventy-five years upon him, and the "Act of Gratuity" as an official valedictory, he would be permitted to enjoy the evening of life in unmolested peace and quiet before his own hearth-stone.

He had been instrumental in influencing the Piscataways toward their choice of an Emperor in 1696. Ochotomoquath had passed, and the tribe was wrangling over his successor, when on September 21, 1704, he was ordered to join Colonel Addison and Colonel Smallwood and inform those Indians that they should agree upon an Emperor to be presented to Governor Seymour at Annapolis for his confirmation, and that at the same time they should be prepared to pay their usual nominal tribute and renew their articles of friendship.

Colonel Beall was appointed Deputy Surveyor for Charles County December 1, 1684, with instructions to lay out ports of entry and trade towns.

On September 15, 1686, he was Town Officer for Mount

Calvert hundred, and on the sixteenth of August, 1692, High Sheriff for Calvert County, a position of prominence and emolument combining nearly all the duties of the present-day county officials, below the judiciary.

Early in 1672 he had a grist mill on Collington branch where he later erected an iron foundry.

Before the landing at Plymouth Rock, Puritanism was a living force in Virginia. Thither went its followers in 1611 settling in Warrasquake, now Nansemond County, where it is said Pocahontas was baptised and married by one of their pastors in 1614. Persecutions arose and in 1649 these religionists with William Durand as Ruling Elder moved to Maryland, settled at the mouth of the Severn river, which they named, and called their united plantations Providence. Out of this settlement grew Anne Arundel County in 1650, and Annapolis, the state capital, in 1695.

Puritanism was sufficiently strong to temporarily change the current of political affairs at the Battle of the Severn in 1655, the year in which Ninian Beall supposedly settled in Maryland.

It does not appear that he became involved in any of the controversies between his coreligionists and Lord Baltimore's representatives though he at once became a factor among them, succeeding Durand as Ruling Elder. Under his guidance the creed flourished on the Western shore of Maryland during the pastorates of Matthew Hill and Nathaniel Taylor from 1668 until 1717.

Although of healthy growth the congregation had no church until on November 20, 1704, Colonel Beall deeded to Nathaniel Taylor a half acre of ground in Upper Marlborough, part of a tract of eighty-two acres, patented December 4, 1694, and known as "The Meadows."

Here a church was erected, and in 1707 he presented the congregation a silver communion service. When the church in Upper Marlborough was abandoned the service was removed to Bladensburg, and subsequently to Hyattsville. Some pieces have been lost, but of the original two chalices and a tankard are preserved.

In 1906 the missing pieces were replaced with this inscription thereon:

"This Server, and these Paten Covers which restore their lost originals, are presented this 20th day of December in the year of Our Lord 1906 to the Hyattsville Presbyterian Church of Hyattsville, Prince George's County, Maryland,
by a great-great-great-great-great-grandson of
Col. Ninian Beall,
Alpheus Benjamin Beall of Sioux City, Iowa.
Presented in recognition of the service of Col. Ninian Beall, Venerable Ruling Elder among the Patuxent Presbyterians before 1700 A. D. who deeded to this Congregation in Upper Marlborough
'A parcell of land' on which to erect its first 'House for the services of Almighty God,' 1704;
who fathered this Congregation and saw it become one of the First seven original Churches
of American Presbyterianism, 1706; and who, in 1707 A. D., gave to this Congregation
this Communion Service, which is now, so far as known, the oldest in use in the Presbyterian Denomination in America."

Probably Ninian Beall's first entry of right to land was made jointly in 1665 in the name of John Boage and Ringing Bell. When the certificate of survey issued the year following it conveyed three hundred acres called "Red Hall" to John Boage and Ninian Bell.

From this date to the time of his death he patented

over twenty-five thousand acres, for which he received certificates of survey for more than thirteen thousand acres, among which were Rock of Dunbarton (795), Bacon Hall (300), Beall's Meadows (1,088), Beall's Choice (690), Collington (300), Edonborough (380), Friendship (600), Good Luck (853), Maiden's Dowry (700), St. Andrews (980), Troublesome (300), Largo (1,031).

Colonel Beall passed his last days on his Bacon Hall plantation adjoining Mount Calvert, the first capital of Prince George's County, about three miles southwest of Upper Marlborough the present county seat. Bacon Hall was granted to him May 1, 1672, and was his home plantation as early as 1686, when he was made Town Officer for Mount Calvert.

His will was executed on January 15, 1717, and probated on February 28, 1717, so that his death occurred between these dates. His remains were possibly buried on his plantation in accordance with the custom of those days, there are indications of an ancient grave-yard on the manor-house portion of Bacon Hall, but they were more probably interred within the confines of the God's half-acre which his christian charity prompted him to give to the Presbyterian congregation in Upper Marlborough, the present site of Trinity Protestant Episcopal church.

Colonel Beall has been pictured with a complection characteristic of his nationality, and an unusually heavy growth of long red hair. Of herculean build considerably over six feet in heighth, powerful in brawn and muscle and phenomenal in physical endurance, a description which he sustained by his spirited activity after the age of more than eighty years.

His wife was Ruth Moore, daughter of Richard and
Jane Moore, a barrister of Calvert County. She died
between 1699, when she was mentioned in the "Act of
Gratuity," and 1704, when she did not join her husband
in his deed of gift to the Presbyterian congregation.

His will mentions sons George, Ninian and Charles;
Mary and Samuel children of son Ninian, deceased;
sons-in-law Joseph Belt and Andrew Hambleton. George
was devised Rock of Dunbarton (408 acres patented for
795), Charles, Dunnback; a thousand-acre tract lying on
the Great Choptank river; Mary and Samuel, Bacon Hall
with the manor-house to the latter who also received his
water-mill and iron-works on Collington branch. Andrew
Hambleton received a slave. Joseph Belt, two hundred
and forty-five acres of Good Luck for a stated consideration to be divided among his heirs, less an open account
for goods, wares and merchandise owed the said Belt.

A tract known as Recovery of four hundred acres
was to be sold in liquidation of outstanding debts.
Charles was bequeathed a work by Bishop Cooper and
he with George and Joseph Belt was directed to purchase
twelve copies of "advice to young & old & middle age,"
by the Reverend Christopher Ness, for distribution among
his grandchildren and godsons.

Traditionally Colonel Beall was the father of twelve
children. He mentions but three of them in his will by
which he devised about two thousand eight hundred
acres of land. Undoubtedly he had previously conveyed
property to other sons and daughters upon their reach-
ing age or marrying.

Unfortunately the records of Calvert, in which county
Colonel Beall lived until 1696, were destroyed by fire in
1882, so that it seems impracticable to secure all of their

names. The most acceptable list includes John, Thomas, died unmarried in England, Ninian, married Elizabeth ——, Captain Charles, married Mary ——, Colonel George, married Elizabeth Brooke, Sarah, married Captain Samuel Magruder, Hester, married Colonel Joseph Belt, Jane, married Colonel Archibald Edmondstone, Mary, married Andrew Hambleton, Margery, married (firstly) Thomas Sprigg, 3d, and (secondly) Colonel Joseph Belt, her sister Hester's widower; Rachael, married —— Offutt, James.

The early records of Maryland identify Colonel Beall by a variety of spelling such as: "Ninian Bale-Ringing, Bell-Ninian, Beale-Ninion, Beale-Ninian, Ninian Bell." He did not sign his will owing to illness, but it is his—marked "Ninian Beall," and he apparently uniformly adopted this style from about 1667.

Some works on heraldry give his arms as:

Sable, a chevron between three wolves' heads erased argent.

Crest—A demi-wolf sable, sustaining a half spear in plain tasseled or.

The proper blazon is:

Arms—Azure a chevron between three bells or.

Crest—A bell or.

When Colonel Beall settled in Maryland in 1655 there were four counties in the province: St. Mary's, Anne Arundel, Kent and Calvert with a population of about ten thousand. Two years before his death (1715) Maryland was the third most populous of the colonies with 50,200 souls, being exceeded by Massachusetts with 96,000 and Virginia with 95,000, and exceeding Connecticut, Pennsylvania including Delaware, New York,

New Jersey, South Carolina, North Carolina, New Hampshire, Rhode Island, and Georgia.

Descendants of Colonel Beall have figured conspicuously in all the wars of our country, and risen to distinction in all the walks of civil life. He was the progenitor of at least four governors of Maryland: Samuel Sprigg, Enoch Louis Lowe, Thomas George Pratt, and Edwin Warfield.

As Georgetonians your greatest interest probably centers in the fact that Colonel Beall was the patentee of Rock of Dunbarton dated November 18, 1703. It was in possession of his son Colonel George Beall and became part of the site of the town when the original survey and plat were completed on February 27, 1752. Two lots each having been assigned to Colonel George Beall and George Gordon those remaining were sold on the 2d of March following " at the house of Joseph Belt, Jr., living in said town," a grandson of Colonel Ninian Beall.

Born of Presbyterian parentage in Harford County, Maryland, Stephen Bloomer Balch, pupil of John Witherspoon and graduate of Princeton in 1774, was captain of a company of militia which several times had a brush with the British during the Revolution. Licensed to preach in 1779 by the Presbytery of Donegal he delivered a sermon in Georgetown and so captivated his hearers by his forcefulness as a pulpit orator and the winsomeness of his personality that he was asked to remain with the promise of a church.

Missionary work in the Carolinas and Georgia first claimed him, but on the 16th of March, 1780, he returned. It is probable that his first sermon following was delivered in a log cabin on High street. Later he used a building at the corner of Bridge and Market streets which served as a school-house on weekdays and a church on Sunday. In 1782 a church was erected on West street which was replaced by the present structure in 1821, Thomas Jefferson, then President, and Albert Gallatin, his Secretary of the Treasury, being among the contributors.

Until the year 1804 Doctor Balch was the only Protestant clergyman in Georgetown. Too much the ideal christian to restrict his ministerial services to the members of his congregation he was a good shepherd to all who needed material aid or craved spiritual comfort. The nearest Episcopal church was St. Paul's, Rock Creek, a chapel of St. John's, Broad Creek, in turn a chapel of St. John's, Piscataway, the mother potential of many churches.

In 1796 the Reverend Walter Dulany Addison, then pastor at Broad Creek, made a determined effort to collect a congregation and build a house of worship in Georgetown. Colonel William Deakins gave the ground, and about 1804 the structure in which we have gathered was sufficiently inclosed to permit of service-holding. It was completed in 1806, and consecrated in 1809.

Through all the years of effort and disappointment preceding its erection Mr. Addison had the cheering assistance of Doctor Balch. When his intentions of founding a parish became known Doctor Balch offered his own church as a place of congregating, continued his interest in the new church project, and made a substantial contribution toward its completion.

All this liberality is but a reflex of that broad christianity which characterized Colonel Ninian Beall when in 1691 he asked to his home the Quaker Thomas Wilson who there remained two nights with him and held a meeting. Wilson in writing of it all the more appreciated the kindnesses extended him because "he was an elder among Presbyterians." Again when Colonel Beall signed a petition to King William III asking that the Church of England become the established church of Maryland.

And it will be still further emphasized this afternoon when a memorial boulder to a Ruling Elder of the Presbyterian church shall be unveiled in an Episcopal church-yard.

The origin and growth of these two denominations in Georgetown trace from Doctor Balch and Mr. Addison. Doctor Balch married Elizabeth Beall, great-granddaughter of Colonel Ninian Beall and in a later generation Colonel Beall's descendants intermarried with those of Mr. Addison. Both of these good souls left their impress for all that is most ennobling and even yet the fragrance of their holy lives is like a benediction.

When the veil is withdrawn from the boulder you may read this inscription on the tablet:

Colonel Ninian Beall
Born Scotland 1625   Died Maryland 1717
Patentee of Rock of Dunbarton
Member of the House of Burgesses
Commander-in-Chief of Provincial Forces of Maryland
In grateful recognition of his services upon all Incursions of Neighbouring Indians the Maryland Assembly of 1699 passed an "ACT OF GRATUITY." Erected by the Society of Colonial Wars in the District of Columbia.
1910.

The inner edge of the border showing a beaded effect, represents wampum; the arrow-heads are modeled after specimens gathered in Georgetown, the site of an Indian village called Tohoga as early as 1608, and are alike true to nature and to history; while the outer edge presents Indian sketch-work indicative of sunshine and shadow.

If the name of him whom we honor today has been long in the shadow of dark forgetfulness, let us hope that the deference here paid him may serve to bring that name into the bright sunshine of a worthy memory, to be illuminated always.

GRANT FOR "BACON HALL," MAY 1, 1672.

CECELIUS Absolute Lord Propry of the Provinces of Maryland and Avalon Lord Baron of Baltimore &c, To all persons to whom these presents shall come Greeting in our Lord God Everlasting

Know yee that we for and in consideracon that Ninian Beale of Calvert County in our sd province of Maryland planter hath due unto him Three hundred Acres of Land within our said province part of a warrant for One Thousand & fifty acres of Land to him granted the Eighteenth day of July last past as appears upon record And upon such Conditions and terms as are Expressed in our Conditions of plantation of our said province of Maryland under our greater Seal at Armes bearing date at London the second day of July in the Year of our Lord God 1649 with such alterations as in them is made by our declaration bearing date the two and twentieth day of September Anno 1658 And Remaining upon record in our said province of Maryland. Do hereby grant unto him the said Ninian Beale all that parcell of land called [Bacon Hall] lying in Calvert County on the West side of the Western Branch of patuxent River, and beginning at a bounded Oak being the South East Corner Tree of the Land of Baker Brooke, Esqr called Brookes Grove, bounded by the said Land And running South West One hundred & sixty perches, to a bounded White Oak, in the Line of the Land of Peter Joy, bounded by the said Joy's Land, and running South East Two hundred and twenty perches, to a bounded pokehikary of the said Joyes Land, and running South West by another Line of the said Joyes Land One hundred and Sixty perches to a bounded poplar of the said Land and running East by South One hundred and twenty perches, to a bounded White oak, of a parcell of Land formerly laid out for Thomas Trueman Esqr bounded by the said Land and from the said Oak running North and by East Seventy five perches to a bounded oak of the said Land, and from thence running still bounded by the said Land East and by South Eighty perches to a bounded Oak of the Land of John Bigger called [Muscle Shell] and

North and by West **Two** hundred and forty perches to a bounded Oak of a parcell of Land formerly laid out for Major Thomas Brooke, called the Grove Landing bounding by the said Land and running West and by North fifty perches to an Oak, and from thence to the first bounded Tree, Containing and now laid out for Three hundred Acres more or less, Together with all rights profits and benefitts thereunto belonging (Royall Mines Excepted) To have and to hold the Same unto him the said Ninian Beale his heirs and assigns forever. To be holden of us and our heirs as of our Mannr of Calverton in free and common Soccage by fealty only for all manner of Services Yielding and paying therefore Yearly unto us and our heirs at our receipt at our City of St. Maries at the two most usuall feasts in the Year Viz At the Feast of the Annunciation of our blessed Virgin Mary and at the feast of Saint Michael the Arch angell by even and equitable portions the Rent of Twelve Shillings Sterling in Silver or gold and for a fine upon every alienacon of the said Land or any part or parcell thereof One Whole years Rent in Silver or gold or the full value thereof in such Comodities as we or our heirs or such officer or officers appointed by us or our heirs from time to time to Collect and Receive the same shall Accept in discharge thereof at the choice of us and our heirs or such officer or officers as afd Provided that if the said Ninian Beale his heirs or assigns shall not pay unto us or our heirs or such officer or officers as afd. the said Sums for a fine before such alien- acon and Enter the said alienacon upon record either in the Provin- ciall Court or in the County Court where the said parcell of Land lyeth within One month next after such alienacon the said alien- acon shall be void and of none effect,—Given at our City of Saint Maries under our great Seal of our said province of Maryland the first day of May in the XXXXth year of our dominion over our sd. province Annoque Domi 1672

Witness our dear Son Charles Calvert Esqr our Capt General and chief Governr of our said province of Maryld

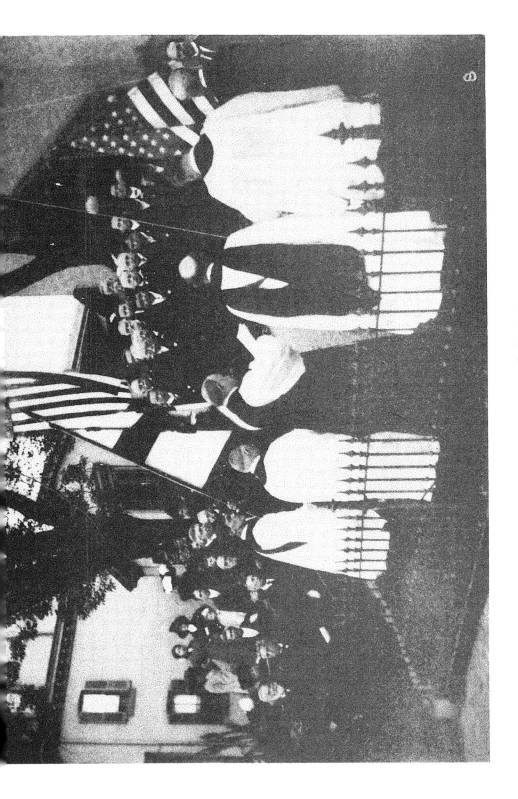

PATENT FOR "ROCK OF DUNBARTON."
NOVEMBER 18, 1703.

CHARLES Absolute Lord propry of the provinces of Mary-land and Avalon Lord Baron of Baltimore &c., To all persons to whom these presents shall come Greeting in our Lord God Everlasting Know yee that for and in consideracon that Ninian Beale of Prince George's County hath due unto him seven hundred and ninety five acres of land within our said province being due unto him by Virtue of a warrant for five hundred acres granted him the nineteenth day of May one thousand seven hundred and two and another warrant for nine hundred and twenty acres granted him the sixth day of May one thousand seven hundred and two as appears in our Land office and upon such Condicons and termes as are expressed in our Condicons of plantacons of our said province bearing date the fifth day of April one thousand six hundred eighty and four and remaining upon record in our said province together with such alteracons as in them are made by our further Condicons bearing date the fourth day of December one thousand six hundred and ninety six and registered in our land office of our said province Wee doe therefore hereby grant unto him the said Ninian Beale all that Tract or parcell of land called Rock of Dunbarton lying in the said county Beginning at the South East Corner Tree of a Tract of land taken for Robert Mason standing by potomeck River side at the mouth of Rock Creek on a point running thence with the said land North North West six hundred and forty ps. thence east three hundred and twenty ps. then south six deg. and a half. Easterly four hundred and eighteen ps. then West one hundred and seventy five ps. then with a streight line by the creek and River to the first bound. Containing and then laid out for seven hundred ninety and five acres more or less according to the Cert. thereof taken and returned into our land Office bearing date of the fourth day of November seventeen hundred and two and there remaining together with all rights profits benefits and priviledges thereunto

(35)

belonging Royall mines excipted To have and to hold the Same
unto him the said Ninian Beale his heirs and assigns forever to be
holden of us and our heirs as of our manor of Calverton in free and
Common Soccage by fealty only for all manner of Services yielding and paying therefore yearly unto us and our heirs at our
receipt at the City of S. Maries at the two most usuall feasts in
the year Viz at the feast of the Annunciacon of the blessed Virgin
Mary and S. Michaell the arch angell. by even and equall porcons
the rent of one pound eleven shills. and nine pence half penny
Ster. in silver or gold and for a fine upon every alienacon of the
said land or any part or parcell thereof one whole years rent in
silver or gold or the full value thereof in such Commodities as
wee and our heirs or such officer or officers as shall be appointed
by us and our heirs from time to time to Collect and receive the
same shall accept in discharge thereof at the choice of us and our
heirs or such officer or officers as aforesaid provided that if the
said Sume for a fine for alienacon shall not be paid to us and our
heirs or such officer or officers as aforesaid before such alienacon
and the said alienacon entered upon Record either in the provin-
ciall Court or in the County Court where the same parcell of land
lyeth within one month next after such alienacon the said alienacon shall be void & of no effect.   Given under our greater Seale
at arms this eighteenth day of November one thousand seven
hundred and three Witness our Trusty and well beloved Coll.
Henry Darnall keeper of our greater scale in our said province of
Maryland

Colonel Ninian Beall's Deed of Gift to the Presbyterian Congregation, Upper Marlborough, Maryland, November 20, 1704.

TO all Christian people to whome these presents shall come I Ninian Beall Senior of Prince Georges County in ye Province of Maryland Send Greeting:

Know yee that I the said Ninian Beall being of a good and perfect minde and without any ffraud or deceipt for divers good Causes and Considerations me thereunto moving but more Especially for ye Propagation of ye Gospell of Christ Jesus, have given, Granted and Confirmed and by these Presents doo ffreely, voluntarily & absolutely give grant and confirme unto Nathaniell Taylor, Minister of ye Gospell to Robert Bradley James Stoddart John Battie Archibald Edmundson Thomas Beall Senior Thomas Beall Junior Ninian Beall Junior Charles Beall Christopher Thompson Joshua Hall John Browne John Henry James Beall Alexander Beall William Ophett John Soaper and to their Successors for ye Erection and Building a House for the service of Almighty God that parcell of land being Part of a Tract of Land called the Meddows Lying on ye Western Branch of Patuxent River in Prince Georges County Beginning at a small Bounded Red Oake near ye North West Corner of the said Meeting house and running East tenn perches then South Eight perches then west tenn perches then north to ye first tree Containing halfe an acre of Land be it more or less To have and to Hold ye said Land and tennaments with their rights member and appurtenances thereunto belonging unto ye said Nathaniell Taylor Robert Bradley James Stoddart John Battie Archibald Edmundson Thomas Beall Senior Thomas Beall Junior Ninian Beall Junior Charles Beall Christopher Thompson Joshua Hall John Browne John Henry James Bell Alexnr Beall William Ophett John Soaper and to their Successors &

and to their Onely Propper use for ye affore Mentioned use &
no other from ye Day of the date hereof forever ffreely Peac-
ably & Quietly without any manner of Reclaime Challenge
or Contradiction of me ye said Ninian Beall my heirs Executors
admns or assigns or of any other Person or Persons by any meanes
title or Procurement in any manner or wise and without any account recoving or answer therefor to me or any in my name to be
given rendred or don in time to Come See ye Neither I the said
Ninian Beall my heirs &c nor any other Person or Persons by us
for us or in our names or in ye names of any of us at any time
hereafter may ask Claime Challenge or demand in or to ye Prom-
ises or any Part thereof any Interest Right title or Possession but
from all action of Right title Claims Interest use possession &
demand thereof wee and Every of us to be utterly Excluded and
forever debarred by these presents, And I the said Ninian Beall
my Heirs &c ye said halfe acre of Land with the appurtenances
unto ye above named Nathaniell Taylor &c and their Successors
for ye use above mentioned against all people will warrant & De-
fend by these presents and I the said Ninian Beall have putt ye
said Nathaniell Taylor &c into peacable possession by the delivery
of a Peice of money Called Six pence whc. I have paid & Dcliv-
ered unto ye said Nath Taylor in behalfe of himselfe and ye rest of
ye above named persons the day & date hereof In Witness
whereof I have hereunto sett my hand & Seale ye 20th day of
November anno 1704

NINIAN BEALL

Signed Sealed and Delivered
In Presens
John Wight
Saml Magruder

LAST WILL AND TESTAMENT OF NINIAN BEALL, EXECUTED JANUARY 15, 1717, PROBATED FEBRUARY 28, 1717.

IN THE NAME OF GOD, AMEN.

I NINIAN BEALL of Prince George's County in the Province of Maryland being indisposed in body but of sound & perfect memory God be praised for the same & considering the Mortality of Human nature and uncertainty of Life doe make ordaine Constitute & appoynt this to be my last Will & Testament in manner and form following Vizt

Impri I give and bequeath my soule into the hands of almighty God in hopes of free pardon for all my Sinns and as for my body to be committed to the Earth from whence it came to be Decently buried at ye discression of my Trustees hereafter named.

Item I will and bequeath that all my Debts and funerall charges be first paid and Satisfied and as for what portion of my Worldly Goods as shall be then Remaining I bequeath & bestow the same in manner following

Item I doe give and bequeath unto my Sonn George my Plantation and tract of Land called the Rock of Dunbarton lying and being att Rock Creeke containing Four Hundred and Eight acres with all the stock thereon both Cattle and Hoggs them and their increase unto my said Sonn George & unto him and his heirs forever.

Item I do allso give and bequeath unto sd son George Beall his choyce of one of my Feather bedds bolster & Pillow and other furniture thereunto belonging with two cows & calves and half my Sheepe from off this Plantation I now live on to him and his heirs forever.

Item I do give and bequeath unto my sonn in Law Andrew Hambleton my Negro Woman Alce unto him his heirs forever.

Item I doe give and bequeath unto my Grandaughter Mary Beall ye Daughter of my Sonn Ninian Beall Deceased the one halfe part of all my Movables or Personall Estate as Cattle &

Hoggs Horses Household goods after my Leagacies before bequeathed are paid and satisfied unto her the said Mary & to her heirs forever.

Item I doe give and bequeath unto my said Grandaughter Mary Beall all yt part of Bacon Hall that lyeth on ye South side of the Road that goeth to Mount Calvert to her the sd Mary & unto her heirs forever.

Item I do give and bequeath unto my grandson Samuel Beall all the remainder part of Bacon Hall togather with the Plantation & orchard & tobacco houses thereto belonging (with this Proviso) that when he comes to age of one and twenty yt that he make over by a Firm Conveyance all his Right and Title yt he hath unto a certain tract of land called Sam's beginning on the South side of the Sd Road going to Mount Calvert unto the sd Mary & unto her heirs forever, but if my said Grandson Should happen to dye before he arrive to be of that age to make over the land soe as aforesaid then I do give and bequeath unto my said Grandaughter Mary ye whole Trackt of Bacon Hall with the houses and orchard thereon unto her and her heirs forever.

Item I doe give and bequeath unto my Said Grandson Samuel Beall my Water Mill Lying upon Collington Branch with the Stones Iron Works Houses & all other materials thereunto belonging unto the sd Samuel and unto his heirs forever.

Item I give and bequeath unto my Son in Law Joseph Belt part of a tract of land called good luck containing two hundred forty-five Acres he allowing unto my heirs ye Sume of four thousand Pounds of Tobacco according to our former agreement he deducting what I doe owe him on his book for Severall Wares & Merchandizes had of him to the said Joseph and unto his heirs forever.

Item that whereas I doe owe Several debts I doe empower my Trustees hereafter named to enable them to pay the same to sell a Certain Tract of Land called the Recovery lying & being in the Freshes of the Patuxent River near the head of the Western Branch to be sold it containeth four Hundred acres, the aforesaid Tract of Land bequeathed unto my Sonn Bellt is adjoining thereto.

Item I do give and bequeath unto my Son Charles Beall a Booke of Bishop Cooper's works the Acts of the Church & the Chronocle of King Charles ye first and King Charles ye Second ye second and I doe hereby request and obleidge my sonn Charles my son Belt and my son George to send for a Dozen of Books intitled an advice to young & old & middle age sett forth by one Mr Christopher Ness ye books to be distributed amongst my Grandchildren & God Sone.

Item I do give and bequeath unto my Sonn Charles a Thousand acres cf Land called Dunnback lying on the South Side of great Choptank in a Creeke called Waltres creek unto him & his heirs forever and Lastly I doe make ordeine declare and appoint my Grandson Samuel Beall to be my Sole and whole Execur of this my last Will and Testament and I do desier my loveing Sonns Charles Beall Joseph Belt and George Beall to doe and perform my Desier as above Exprest and to act and doe for my Executor untill he arrive to the age of one and twenty hereby revoaking and annulling all former and other Wills by me att any time heretofore made and signed and doe desier my said Sonns to use their best care and indeavor that my two Grandchildren the children of my beloved Sonn Ninian Beall Deceased be brought and have their Education Suitable to ther Esteate and I doe alsoe appoynt and desier my said Sonns Trustees to this my Will to make their appearance every easter Tuesday or any other time as they shall think a more fitting time att my Dwelling Plantation yearly to inspect into all affaires thereof and of a yearly increase of all the Creatures upon my Plantation and att the Mill for and on the behalfe of my two Grandchildren who are to be Joynt Sharers therein my grandaughter to have her part at ye day of Marriage.

In Testimony whereof I have to this my last Will & Testament Sett my hand and Seale this fifteenth day of January in the Yeare of Our Lord God one thousand and seven Hundred and Seventeen.

the mark of
Ninian   X   Beall (Seal)

LIST OF PUBLICATIONS OF THE SOCIETY OF COLONIAL WARS IN THE DISTRICT OF COLUMBIA, ORGANIZED MAY 20, 1893.

Register of the Society. 1897. With portrait of Richard Worsam Meade, Rear-Admiral, U.S.N. pp. 124.

Register of the Society. 1904. With frontispiece of badge of the Society of Colonial Wars, portrait of Francis Asbury Roe, Rear-Admiral, U.S.N., First Governor of the Society, and other officers. Twenty-two portraits. pp. 214.

MEMORIAL PAPERS.

No. 1. George Brown Goode. By A. Howard Clark. With portrait. pp. 8. 1896.

No. 2. Charles Frederick Tiffany Beale. By Marcus Benjamin. With portrait. pp. 13. 1902.

No. 3. William Herman Wilhelm, Captain, U.S.A. By Ethan Allen Weaver. With portrait. pp. 9. 1902.

No. 4. Francis Asbury Roe, Rear-Admiral, U.S.N. By Marcus Benjamin. With portrait and eight other illustrations. pp. 35. 1903.

No. 5. Gilbert Thompson. By Marcus Benjamin. With portrait. pp. 18. 1910.

No. 6. Frederic Wolters Huidekoper. By Frederic Louis Huidekoper. With portrait, chronology, notices and resolutions. pp. 42. 1910.

HISTORICAL PAPERS.

No. 1. The Colonial Boundaries of Virginia and Maryland. By Gilbert Thompson. With map. pp. 8. 1899.

No. 2. An American Sea Captain of Colonial Times. By Francis Asbury Roe, Rear-Admiral, U.S.N. pp. 11. 1900.

No. 3. Historical Military Powder-horns. By Gilbert Thompson. With eleven illustrations. pp. 16. 1901.

No. 4. Historical Address at Dedication of the Braddock Boulder, Nov. 10, 1907. By Marcus Benjamin. With four illustrations. pp. 16. 1908.

No. 5. Colonel Joseph Belt. By Caleb Clarke Magruder, Jr. With Patent and illustration of "Chevy Chase" manor-house. pp. 36. 1909.

No. 6. Historical Address at Dedication of the Colonel Ninian Beall Boulder, October 30, 1910. By Caleb Clarke Magruder, Jr.

With six illustrations, Grant for "Bacon Hall," Patent for "Rock of Dunbarton," Deed of Gift to Patuxent (Md.) Congregation, and Colonel Beall's Will. pp. 44. 1911.

MISCELLANEOUS.

Address of Welcome, by his Excellency, Governor Francis A. Roe, U.S.N., at first dinner of the Society, December 19, 1893. pp. 8.

Preliminary draft of a Constitution, printed upon half-sheets and sent to members for suggestions. pp. 18. November, 1894.

The preceding was adopted and printed in February, 1895. A circular of four pages, with preamble and qualifications for membership, was printed, 1895; also, a similar circular, giving list of members, was printed January, 1896.

A list of membership is published annually as a circular. pp. 4.

The Year Book and Register of the Society, 1897, contains the Constitution and By-Laws as amended to that date.

Preliminary draft of Constitution, printed and sent to members for suggestions. With cover. pp. 17. April, 1902.

The preceding was adopted without change, May 13, 1902, and printed, with embossed seal of the Society on the cover. pp. 16.

First Service, Sunday, February 12, 1905. St. John's Church, Georgetown, D. C. (With embossed seal.) pp. 12.

Second Annual Service, Sunday, February 18, 1906. St. John's Church, Washington. (With embossed seal.) pp. 12.

Third Annual Service, Sunday, February 17, 1907. Epiphany Church, Washington. (Without seal.) pp. 12.

Dedication service, Sunday, November 10, 1907. Cathedral Grounds, D. C. One illustration of the Braddock tablet and boulder. pp. 12.

Fourth Annual Church Service, Sunday, April 26, 1908. Christ Church, Georgetown, D. C. (Without seal.) pp. 8.

Fifth Annual Church Service, Sunday, May 2, 1909. St. John's Church, Washington. (Without seal.) pp. 9.

Sixth Annual Church Service, Sunday, May 8, 1910. St. John's Church, Washington. (Without seal.) pp. 9.

Dedication Service, Sunday, October 30, 1910. Colonel Ninian Beall memorial. St John's Church, Georgetown, D. C. With illustration of tablet and boulder. pp. 10.

CALEB CLARKE MAGRUDER, Jr.,

Historian.

January 27, 1911.

Made in the USA
Middletown, DE
11 March 2021